BRAND REPPIN' 101

BECOME A BRAND REP IN 60 DAYS

by
Angel N. Livas

DC MEDIA CONNECTION *PUBLISHING*
500 Montgomery St, Suite 400, Alexandria, VA 22314

Copyright © 2018 by Angel N. Livas
All rights reserved.

LIBRARY OF CONGRESS CATALOGING - IN - PUBLICATION DATA
Livas, Angel
Brand Reppin' 101: Become A Brand Rep In 60-Days
1. Business 2. Parenting
2018902279

ISBN: 978-0-692-07392-6

Printed and bound in the United States of America
First Printing March 2018

Excerpt from article in entrepreneur.com by Derek Newton. Reprinted with permission.
Edited by Deb Long & Shamaila Iqebal
Front Cover Image Created by DC Media Connection, LLC
All photographs by Angel Livas, unless otherwise credited in book
Book design by DC Media Connection, LLC

Published by DC Media Connection

Follow: @angelnlivas | @livasboys | @livasboysdesigns | @dcmediaconnect

Visit: www.angelnlivas.com | www.livasboys.com | www.dcmediaconnection.com

Table of Contents

About The Author

Angel Livas is a Gracie Award-Winning Executive Producer, a Multi-Media Personality, the President and CEO of DC Media Connection, LLC, the Chief Engagement Officer of Creative Introduction, LLC and the Founder of The Woman Behind The Business Nonprofit, Retreat, and Talk Show.

With nearly two-decades of media experience, Angel believes in sharing her wealth of multi-media expertise to help propel the success of others. In 2016, Angel was highlighted in the Washington Business Journal under "People On The Move" and named "Influential Business Woman of 2016" by AI Magazine. Prior to launching her small businesses, Angel oversaw six-nationally syndicated talk-radio shows, which included producing programming for award-winning celebrity hosts: Larry King & Jane Pauley.

Angel has continuously expanded audience reach, enhanced member engagement and increased brand recognition by crafting original content for web, radio, and social media. She launched her career in Washington, DC, as an intern at WHUR – 96.3 FM, and has come full circle to now host "The Woman Behind The Business" Talk Show on WHUR-96.3 FM - HD4. She has worked at such esteemed media outlets as Bloomberg Television, NBC and AARP, where she spent a decade and was ultimately the Executive Director of their Radio Department.

Angel has completed two certificate programs (Advanced Project Management, Stanford University; Mini-MBA: Social Media Marketing, Rutgers University) after receiving her Master's degree at The American University, with an emphasis in Interactive Journalism. She graduated Magna Cum Laude from Howard University, receiving her Bachelor of Arts in Broadcast Journalism. Angel is a proud lady of Alpha Kappa Alpha Sorority, Incorporated and resides in Northern Virginia with her husband and two children.

Acknowledgements

My journey to parenthood was a road that left much to be desired. Every experience and every lesson deepened my appreciation of what it would mean to be your mother. Noah & Nelson, you are my inspiration and constant reminder of what life is all about.

Mommy loves you!

Preface

Timing is everything. Two months ago, I would have never guessed that I would end up writing a book about Brand Reppin', something I knew absolutely nothing about. Fast-forward until now, and I feel like a seasoned veteran!

So, what's my story? Well, it's short, sweet and simple.

On August 5, 2017 - I ended up working late at my downtown Washington, DC office. My husband suggested that he and the kids join me for dinner near my office. Once they arrived we walked to a nearby restaurant and I noticed that every few feet, people would stop and tell me how adorable my two sons are. It's funny because, now that I'm reflecting - people have always admired Noah & Nelson but, clearly I had never paid it much attention. However, after dinner something triggered me to move from just saying "thank you" to actually building a brand around their "look".

As we began preparing to leave the restaurant, an older woman approached the boys and told them how adorable and well-behaved they were. It was in that moment that I thought – "Hey, if people think enough to stop and tell these kids how cute (and "well-behaved") they are…maybe they will stop and 'like' their pictures on social media?"

Photo Credit: Arocho Apparel

From that simple gesture and "What If" moment the #LivasBoys brand was created.

In this book, I will share how I took the @LivasBoys brand from zero social media presence and no "Brand Repping" knowledge to the boys becoming Brand Reps and Brand Enthusiasts for nearly a dozen brands. I'll also share how they garnered over 600 Instagram followers in under 60 days.

The best part about this book is that many of the techniques that you'll learn can be applied to your personal pages, company pages, etc.

A Brand.... *What*
Brand Rep 101

"When you have dynamic Brand Reps supporting your brand and eagerly sharing discounts, product launches, etc... it shows in product sales."

~ Livas Boys Designs

If the phrase "Brand Rep" or "Brand Enthusiast" is new to you, don't think you're out of the loop. Until I created my kids IG page and started using strong hashtags (hashtags used frequently) I had never heard of the references either.

Brand Representatives (i.e. Brand Reps) and Brand Enthusiasts are individuals contracted to share images of themselves promoting products in exchange for receiving the items at a discount or completely free from small shops (small businesses that sell products on sites like ETSY).

According to an article titled "So What's a Brand Ambassador and Why Are They Important?" on Entrepreneur.com - the author explains that "For most businesses, especially startups, getting the word out about you and your product is essential. And there are many ways to do it but in the most general terms, everything you do to raise your profile and sell your products will fall into one of three categories: Advertising, Marketing or Public Relations." The author goes on to say "...a Brand Ambassador is a person who's tried your product or service and loves it -- loves it enough to say amazing things about it." And as a Brand Rep - that's essentially your role. You have to really stand behind the product - share news about the shop that you're representing and their products, sales, and of course pictures of you (or the person's account you're managing) Repping the brand.

There is a huge community of small shops that utilize Brand Reps and Enthusiasts on Instagram and Facebook to help raise awareness of their products or services organically. At this point you might be wondering, "What's the difference between a Brand Rep and Brand Enthusiast?"

Typically, I equate Brand Reps and Enthusiasts as social media models. But, here is how they differ:

Brand Reps often receive their clothing or products completely free or at a higher discounted rate than Enthusiasts. Often times the differentiator between the category into which individuals are placed have to do with the photo quality of the images that currently exist on that persons social media platform. Another determining factor, is whether the company believes your style aligns with their brand, which can possibly weigh heavier than picture quality at times.

I look at the Brand Enthusiast's role as "still in training". This group is often held to the same contractual obligations as Brand Reps - but, they do not receive the same level of perks. Some companies, however, might provide an opportunity for Enthusiast's to earn free items, although, it's not guaranteed.

Both groups are highly respected and appreciated by the small shops they represent. And because the slots are limited - it's truly a privilege to be selected to be in either category. Trust me, I've seen hundreds of people put their name in the hat...but, only a few are chosen.

End of Chapter 1 Questionnaire:

Do you think Brand Repping is for you or your family?:

____

____

____

What benefits of Brand Repping most interest you?

____

____

____

What aspects of being a Brand Enthusiast appeal to you?

____

____

____

Getting Started
Building your brand from the ground up!

"It is … very important that reps take my business and their title seriously…"
~ *The Sassy Touch*

Like most things… you get out of Brand Repping what you're willing to put into it. But, if you don't know where you should be focusing your attention or exactly what you should be putting into it...keep reading. In this chapter you'll gain step by step guidance to help you attract brands for various opportunities, as well as gain the attention of other Brand Reps for collaborations.

STEP 1
Build Your Platform

Some shops might not mind you wanting to promote your son or daughter's Brand Repping pictures on your personal social media pages - but, I am going to treat this as any other business venture and strongly encourage you to create a special account to build your platform as a Brand Rep.

I know it might seem easier to just post pictures on your existing account - but, think about what your personal page previously represented and what your audience was accustomed to receiving from you. If you start flooding your page with pics of your little one (no matter how adorable he or she might be) or company products that you're repping for, people will more than likely start unfollowing you. It's not to say that they don't like kids or the products you're promoting - but, a lot of times people decide to follow their friends, co-workers or perfect strangers based on what they believe they can count on receiving from that individual. If you decide to start changing it up on them...they will more than likely just quietly unfollow you and you will begin to see your numbers decrease.

On the other hand - you also want to market yourself as a serious Brand Rep to potential small shops. You'll be amazed by the community that you'll be joining and you want people to know exactly what they can expect when they see your profile name and pictures that appear in their social media feed...great content!

When your brand is consistent, you are better equipped to grow your audience organically.

STEP 2
Create Your Account Profile

Once you decide to establish a unique identity for your brand - you're probably thinking, "Now what"? The next step is   to ensure that your profile information aligns with the purpose of your   page. Your social media handle (i.e. @yoursocialmedianame) is how others will connect with you and identify you. For example: if you personally like tutu's and are considering it for your handle - yet you're building an image for your twin boys - the naming might be misleading (unless of course that's what you're going for... then by all means). The point here is to just be sure that your social media handle / profile name reflects the image that you want to portray to your audience.

The same is true for your profile picture; nothing portrays the image of your brand like a picture. So, consider posting an image of something that reflects your brand over merely posting a graphic. Here's some food for thought, you might love your logo - but, people relate more to people. That's why I always recommend selecting a nice picture over a graphic.

When it comes to completing your bio don't over think it. If you are interested in Brand Repping or Enthusiast opportunities, state it. Just consider how you currently experience other people's profiles. If you rarely read them, other people probably rarely read yours. However, companies seeking out new talent will more than likely peruse bios and completed profiles, along with individuals seeking collaboration opportunities.

STEP 3
Imagery - keep it clear

One of the requirements small shops look for when selecting Brand Reps is the photographer's (mom or dad typically) ability to capture clear and uncluttered images. You don't have to take the kids to a portrait studio or anything fancy - just be creative. Some brands have background stipulations or preferences - while others just want clear images of their products in use.

Whatever you do...just keep it simple...and clear.

The less noise (distractions) in the background of your shots will increase the viewer's attention to the products of the small shops. Keep in mind - these shops might think your kids are adorable but, they don't benefit if you aren't able to capture clear images of their products. Check out the example below. When I'm taking pictures of my kids - I let them be themselves. I hate overly posed images because they have the tendency to look "forced". At times it takes a little longer to get the perfect shot...but, oh - once you've captured it - you know it!

In Example 1. Mommy was trying to get the kids to stand up straight and just say cheese. As you can see - one said cheese - while looking off camera, and the other one served up a cute pout. Now, while we did use this image - we made sure we provided additional images that showcased the boys in their true element.

In Example 2. The boys were merely playing around and happened to capture, what I consider to be the perfect snapshot. The lighting was dynamic - their energy transfers through the image... and most importantly it looks fun, clean and clutter free!

Example 1.

Example 2.

End of Chapter 2 Questionnaire:

Where will you start? As you begin thinking about ways in which to build your profile, use the space below to brainstorm profile names:

____

____

____

____

It's time to select your profile image…what look or feel do you want your page to portray? Describe a few different vibes you would want people to experience when they stop at your page?

____

____

____

____

Draft a sample IG bio…remember to keep it simple. What's the most important information for your target audience?

____

____

____

____

Locating Brand Rep Opportunities

It's not as hard as it might seem

Some people like to take their time and learn as much as possible before they take on new adventures -- while others plunge in and learn as they go. Whichever best describes your learning style, this chapter will provide you with practical advice to get your "Brand Rep" ball rolling.

If you've completed all of the Steps that we discussed in earlier Chapters, such as:

1. Designating account just for "modeling"

2. Completing your profile

3. Choosing images for your page that are crisp and free from clutter

4. Actively engaging on social media (i.e posting frequently, responding to posts, etc.)

...you are ready to go!
If you don't have a lot of followers yet, don't worry about that at the moment... we'll get there in the next Chapter.

When the Livas Boys first started inquiring about Brand Rep opportunities - we had less than 100 followers. Initially, I would find shops that I liked and I would introduce the boys and share their IG page information. This is a slower process for results - but, we definitely had a few shops pick up the Livas Boys - even when they might not have been in their "Brand Rep Search" season. What's that you might ask?

Well, the same way modeling agencies host model calls and Broadway hosts casting calls… small shops hold Brand Rep searches to find their newest additions to their teams. In a nutshell here's how it works:

Small Shops posts a social media announcement stating a time period for which interested individuals can enter to be considered for any of their promotional modeling openings. Again these positions are typically Brand Rep, Brand Enthusiast, and on occasion, the Brand Fan roles. Each position provides different discounts and responsibilities...so, it's very important to note which role you're selected for and fulfill your roles accordingly. Some shops will post the perks associated with the title in the Brand Rep search description - while others might not announce benefits until the team has been formed - but, every shop posts instructions for entry.

It is imperative that you follow all of the directions if you want to be considered. A lot of these shops receive hundreds of inquiries - yet, they might only be looking for 6 new team members. Sometimes something as simple as following directions might be the boost you need to be selected.

I can remember the very first shop we were asked to Brand Rep for. I was in complete shock when I received a direct message (DM) from a shop letting me know that we had been selected to join their Brand Rep team. I wasn't in shock because the boys were selected. I think I was in shock because they did not have a lot of followers. When you embark upon something like Brand Repping, you sometimes think that popularity has something to do with it...and it might...but, our first few opportunities definitely knocked that idea completely out the window. We were the new kids on the block and no one knew who we were...but, we were still given a chance.

End of Chapter 3 Questionnaire:

What are some ways to find Brand Repping opportunities?

____

____

____

____

Remember to build your page brand as you go...you don't have to have a wide array of followers to jumpstart Brand Repping. What can you do at this very moment to increase visibility to your page?

____

____

____

____

I'm A Brand Rep...Now What?
Let's do it again!

You know that sense of confidence you experience when you're feeling yourself? It's almost like your inner self is screaming "Yeeessss...I did that." That's exactly how I felt when the boys received their first Brand Repping gig. Everyone's reaction will vary, but one things for certain... once all the excitement has settled it's time to get to work!

From our experience most shops will shoot you a direct message letting you know that you have been selected to join their team. Some follow-up with a contract, while others merely invite you to join their private groups. Whatever the terms of your contract are - be sure to review it thoroughly - and follow through. Please don't be that person who goes through all of the steps to get the gig - but, doesn't follow through. Pay special attention to purchase requirements. Not all shops have purchase requirements but, some do, so you want to make sure you take notes on what you've agreed to, at each level.

The Livas Boys use a cloud based notepad to manage the various requirements we must fulfill for every small shop contract. This document is also helpful when posting images... and you need to locate your discount code to promote special offers.

When promoting or showcasing your child in their branding role, you should always provide their special discount code in the caption or on the graphic. Small shops almost always provide you with a special discount code to share with your followers. Remember, this is a business. You should always include the shop's social media handle within your post's captions. This small trick will make it very simple for people to access the shop's social media page to learn more about their products or services.

Third Party Platforms To Make Your Content Soar

When it comes to the work you produce - If you typically like to go above and beyond to set yourself apart from others…you should consider these two platforms: Adobe Creative Suite Lightroom (must have Adobe account to access) and Canva a free branding & graphic design platform.

In earlier Chapters, we provided pointers to assist you in capturing the perfect shot…but, what we haven't talked about is software to assist with enhancing your shots. For my avid photo editors who use Photoshop or other high performing platforms, this memo may not be for you. But, if you're seeking a simple way to modify your amateur to semi-professional images… Lightroom is a wonderful place to begin. This program is easy to use and can enhance your photos from mediocre to amazing.

One of my favorite graphic design platforms is Canva. Canva allows you to customize your images by adding logos, text, pictures, etc. You can access the free app from your app store, as it is available on both android devices and iOS platforms.

End of Chapter 4 Questionnaire:

A cloud based notebook is a great way to keep track of your term requirements? What are some key elements you should be tracking?

____

____

____

____

What are some good third party applications that can assist you on your Brand Reppin' journey?

____

____

____

____

Gaining Followers
Build your community of Brand Rep Friends!

"When I'm looking for a team
I look for social (media) activity!
- Dazzled In Distress

While it's nice to post awesome pictures…it's even better knowing that other people agree that your pic is pretty dope. I don't believe that anyone would grow angry if hundreds or thousands of people started liking their pictures or even leaving positive comments. As a whole, I think society enjoys social media because of the instant gratification it can provide. Parents gain a sense of pride when they watch their children's likes increase from day-to-day! Now, I'm not calling anyone vain...I'm just saying - we like to know that our "artistry" is appreciated...and what better way for your social media audience to show appreciation than taking the time to leave a comment, click a heart or, by golly - follow you!

Having a huge following is not necessarily a requirement by small shops seeking Brand Reps or Enthusiasts. Per our earlier Chapter - they are seriously most interested in picture quality. But, as a serious entrepreneur, mompreneur or dadpreneur - you should always be thinking about other potential opportunities your page can provide. Growing up, my dad always told me to never depend on just one opportunity - you must always look for other ways to generate revenue...so, I'm going to share that same wisdom with you.

Is Your Content Engaging?

Anyone can snap a picture - but, does your caption make your picture come alive? If not, it should. One of the things I always do before posting a picture of my Brand Reps is get in tune with what I feel the individual is serving up...what are they saying with their expression, attitude, body language, etc. So, check out the sample posts used on the @LivasBoys IG page.

Example 1.2

In each of the examples provided the text supports the image and makes it more compelling, relatable or just plain fun!

Now, I don't want you to panic if you're not an amazing writer...you don't have to be.

None of the captions in any of my posts are award-winning synopses or short stories...they're merely my interpretation of what I felt the image expressed.

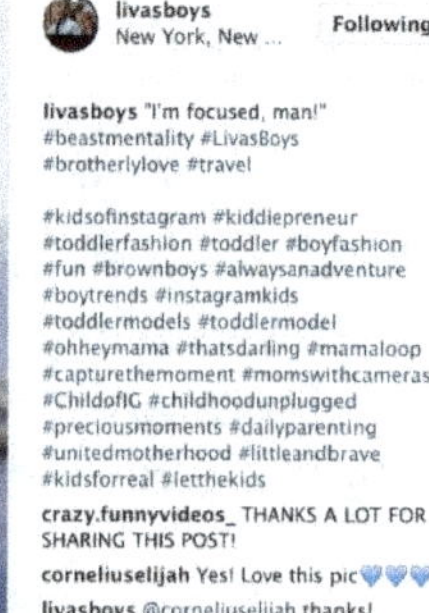

Example 2.1

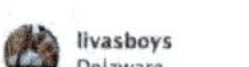

Example 3.1

Example 4.1

At the end of the day - the caption allows you to seal the deal...and provide additional information - while keeping it fun!

For instance, example 3.1 captures 3 boys outside with festive fall decorations as the backdrop... one appears to be screaming - while the others are smiling with glee. The caption reads: "A good ole fall morning... some of us love 'em... some of us don't". In that particular picture we were merely posting engaging content. But, in example 1.1 we're providing information about a particular brand so we "mentioned" - @distrisseddenimpress in our caption. When you want to alert a brand that you're giving them a "shout out" you should always tag them and mention them in your post.

Another example, which showcases that your caption doesn't have to say anything profound is example 2.1. This image captures my son, Nelson deep in thought...it merely states "I'm focused, man" (followed by our hashtags of course)! So, don't beat yourself up trying to find the "perfect" caption - just state one of the first things that come to mind when you see the image…and if applicable, a call to action (i.e. directions for the viewers - for example - visit the link in our bio to learn more)! Other than that - keep it simple, have fun, and enjoy engaging with your audience.

Hashtags
Have you noticed the series of words and phrases used on social media in conjunction with the pound sign or "the hashtag" (#)? Well, in the event you had not noticed, you can scan through previous pictures in this book to check out how we use hashtags. You can integrate hashtags into your post caption, provide a string of hashtags at the end of your caption or post your hashtags separately in the comments section. However you decide to incorporate your hashtags it's cool - just as long as they're a part of your post.

To alleviate conjuring up key words or phrases each time you post your hashtags - consider creating a core group of hashtags and saving them to your phone's notepad. For the most part you will have a consistent group of hashtags that you'll want to include in your posts, but on some occasions you might want to add specific hashtags based on the image, which is totally fine too. Now, just in case you're curious as to why I specifically noted to save your hashtags in your phone - well, for my absolute newbies to

InstaGram - currently, you cannot post images from a computer. You can only post content from your mobile device. So, I save my core hashtags to the notes app on my phone and retrieve them whenever I make a new post, to save me time and *brain power.*

Why Use Hashtags?

Most people have no idea why hashtags are so important - they see other people use them and so they just hashtag any and everything...but, the truth of the matter is - hashtags are used to aggregate content under a particular category. What category you might ask? Whatever your hashtag says. So, if you flip back to the previous page - I always use #kiddiepreneur - this hashtag allows anyone interested in kid entrepreneur's to come across images of the Livas boys. If they like what they see - my bio provides the necessary information for those individuals to follow up and learn more about the boys.

Now, how do hashtags help you gain followers? Well, if your content is engaging and people are merely looking at images under a particular hashtag and it captures their attention enough to click to your page, they will either scroll through your page and go back to perusing content under that hashtag - or they will follow your page before returning. Of course we aim for the latter to occur!

Lastly, it's also a great idea to check out the hashtags other reps are using, as there might be a popular hashtag that you may not be aware of that might be worth adding to your core group of tags. Be sure to check out our core hashtags in the references chapter.

Follow Loops

I'm going to be honest - I had never heard of a follow loop until I started managing a social media account for my kids. And to be even more transparent, I was leery of them - because I didn't want to just follow brands I wasn't interested in. But, here's what happened … as a Brand Rep I realized that I needed to appeal to different groups of people and a Follow Loop allows you to do just that.

Now, if you have no idea what a follow loop is...it is essentially a posting that goes up that might say - Brand Rep Follow Loop - with instructions of how the loop works in the image caption. So, it might tell you to repost the image and follow all of the people in the loop and in return they are supposed to follow you back! Now, you might be thinking - what if they don't actually follow back. Well, you can either continue following them - or you can grab the unfollowers app (can be found in your phone's app store) and unfollow all of the people who are not following you. Pretty simple.

Follow Loops are a great way to build your own "like minded community" while supporting small shops, and other Brand Reps who share their content, information and of course images.

(Graphic example for Brand Rep Follow Loop)

Facebook Groups

If you are reading this book, my guess would be that you have some type of social media presence. So, Facebook Groups should not be unfamiliar to you. Just as you might belong to a closed book club group or have a family group - there are private Brand Rep groups. To locate them - merely search for "Brand Rep", or you can be more specific and aggregate groups for "beginner Brand Reps". You will be surprised by how large the Small Shops and Brand Rep world really is.

Telegram

Have you been invited to participate in a Telegram? Telegram is a free communication app that can be downloaded from your app store. If you're familiar with WhatsApp, the platforms are very similar - although a number of small shops and Brand Reps utilize the application to encourage engagement. How so? Well, you may receive an invitation to join a group that will require you to like images posted (from a certain time period) in their telegram feed (which is a compilation of varying group members posts). For example, one telegram that the Livas Boys belong to requires you to like all of the postings that occurred within the previous 12-hours, before you're permitted to post your individual image. While it can be a tedious process - these telegram communities can host up for 50,000 people - so, your visibility can drastically improve, just from participating. You can find a handful of telegrams that we're aware of in the references Chapter.

End of Chapter 5 Questionnaire:

What can you do to ensure your content is engaging?

____

____

____

____

What are some of the benefits of using hashtags?

____

____

____

____

Can you come up with 3 relevant hashtags for your content?

____

____

____

____

Do follow loops or telegrams sound appealing to you? Why, or why not?

____

____

____

What Small Shops Look For?
In their words...not ours!

By now, I hope you feel like you've gained a lot of insight from the Brand Reps perspective. However, you might be left wondering, "What do the small shops have to say? - since they are the decision makers!" So, I reached out to some of the companies with which the @LivasBoys launched their Brand Repping career to bring you the following...

The first small shop that I'm going to introduce you to is pretty unique. The owner of Arocho Apparel, is Alyssa, a 16-year old High School Student from Virginia. In this next section Alyssa reiterates several points that were made throughout the book. So, get your notepad ready and be prepared to learn and grow your Brand Reppin' opportunities.

In Alyssa's Words

Small shop owners are mostly stay at home moms who don't work because they have little ones, or require another source of income. In my case, I'm a 16-year-old high school hobbyist who is looking for an opportunity in the fashion world. While small shop owners are passionate about what we do, and every creation we make, we need help getting our name out there and that's where the Brand Rep community comes in.

Brand Reps can be highly effective in growing small businesses on Instagram because they help grow the shop's following organically. Small shop owners usually offer free or discounted products in exchange for an agreement that the Brand Rep will provide high-quality photos to be used by the shop on any or all social media platforms, websites and marketing prints. Reps must be active on their social media accounts, and engaging with the brand they are soliciting, while also being willing to share information about brand sales, giveaways and new product releases etc.

Why do we need Brand Reps?

- We are looking to reach a large audience to increase our exposure
- We need product testing and reviews
- We need people with great photography skills
- We need well-styled Product photos
- Bring in New followers and sales

How we select our Reps:

Please keep in mind that we are not in search of the cutest baby, so please don't be offended if your baby is not chosen. All babies/kids are beautiful but might not be a fit for what we need.

What we look for are as follows:

- **Love the label:** Having a love and passion for my label whether you are a supporter on social media by engaging: liking, commenting, or sharing. I search for those who show that they truly love handmade and small shop businesses, and are not just looking for free items.

- **Photo Quality:** One of the most important requirements to becoming a Rep is producing great quality photos. You don't need to buy an expensive DSLR camera, however, it is a great advantage if you do. But, newer phones like the iPhone also works great. All you need to do is: utilize good Natural lighting, keep Filters to a minimum, and make sure that your subject and the product are in focus.

- **Active public account:** Reps must have an active Public account on social media, must be posting at least every other day, most Brand reps post multiple times on a daily basis. The gallery must be active and clean (No advertising of sex, drugs, violence, etc) that's a no-no for me as you will be representing my label. It's also not attractive to see feeds full of competition, entries and lack personality.

- **Style:** Your gallery is a representation of who you are. Your style and wardrobe will be taken into consideration to see if you make a great fit. We look for style and creativity and a large diverse body of Urban and lifestyle wardrobe displayed in your gallery. Your style must fit our brand aesthetic.

- **Followers:** A large follower account is great to have, but do I take that into consideration when choosing my reps NO, a large number of followers in the thousands does not make anyone a better Rep, a customer with hardly any followers can be more effective and supportive of my business because they actually love your label and your product, and sharing it on their social media platform will truly come from the heart.

- **Rep:** Short for Representative: Someone who represents and helps promote a small shop on Instagram and other social media. Being a Rep can be a lot of fun, you get to spend quality time with your little ones and watch them grow into lil fashionistas, meet new people, and build friendships with many boss ladies.

Brand Reppin' can be a great experience, but it is not for everyone. It takes a lot of time, and hard work to help these businesses grow. If you are in it just for the sole purpose of receiving freebies and discounted products then this is not for you. Thank you to all the Rep moms and my Rep family for all you have done for me and continue to do.

Alyssa
www.instagram.com/arocho.apparel

"When I'm looking for a team I look for social activity! Someone who likes to post a lot and support my brand. I also look for their style. My brand is more of an "edgy" style, so I seek that kind of styling from my rep moms! And as far as importance of taking my shop seriously...that's a huge deal. My rep searches bring in more than 300 entries, so if people aren't willing to comply with the terms, I have plenty of people waiting for a spot. It's a big deal."

Dazzled In Distress

"I like to look for diversity in a team. I love to feature all, and show anyone can be a model - no matter what they look like."

"It's very important for Brand Reps to take the opportunity seriously. I work hard to come up with new styles and I need all reps to take it as seriously as I do. I put my heart and soul into my shop and I need reps that feel the same way."

Distressed Denim Press
www.instagram.com/distressed_denim_press

"As a small shop I look for people who are first and foremost truly interested in the items I make, and my brand. When this occurs they are always excited for new items that arrive in my shop. Also I love them being upbeat, positive and very active on social media. I also appreciate very open communication. I am human, so I understand that life happens - so, if they communicate their problems, needs, and wants - it makes working with them a lot easier!"

"It is also very important that reps take my business and their title seriously...as we are doing each other a favor. As I stated previously, life happens and I definitely understand that! However, communication should be open on both sides and most of all, everyone should have fun! I love seeing new faces and my products on other children. It makes me excited and gives me motivation to keep going!"

The Sassy Touch
www.instagram.com/thesassytouch/

"Consistency is key. As a small shop - when you have dynamic Brand Reps supporting your brand and eagerly sharing discounts, product launches, etc… it shows in product sales. The same is true for Brand Reps who aren't as supportive...it impacts your bottom line, because every discount or complimentary product comes at a cost. We work hard to provide our Brand Reps with everything they need to be successful...because when they succeed we both win!"

Livas Boys Designs
www.instagram.com/livasboysdesigns/

End of Chapter 6 Questionnaire:

Based on what small shops look for, what are some things you can start doing to capture the attention of small shops?

____

____

____

____

Do you feel you have a well-versed understanding of how important the Brand Reppin' role is to the small shops they represent?

____

____

____

____

How serious of a commitment is Brand Reppin'?

____

____

____

____

Brand Reps & Kiddie Models
(T)winning!

It's one thing to learn and implement the brand strategies that you've gained from this book...but, we also want to encourage you to think beyond the norm. Dream bigger! So, we're going to share a recent conversation we had with a mom who successfully transitioned her twin boys from adorable IG models to paid models.

It's totally random how I met Temeka Paige, the single mother of twins, Nasir Abrahiem Paige and Jayce Kenneth Paige out of Northern Virginia. We were both attending a networking event and I swear - there were less than 5 people in the venue. I was totally turned off because my friend and I had rushed to get there...and to arrive to such a small turnout was a bummer. But, I didn't let it distract me from taking the time to meet the handful of attendees.

Temeka was the second person that I spoke with and within 2-minutes of speaking with her I realized why I was there. Initially she shared information with me about her event planning company - but, slowly moved into the fact that she manages her two boys as a "momprenuer"! When she said that - my interest was all the way piqued! Here is a snapshot of our conversation...in Q & A form.

1. What are the names and ages of your twin boys?
Nasir Abrahiem Paige and Jayce Kenneth Paige 7yrs old

2. Did your boys or do they work as Brand Reps? If so, how did they get started?
Yes, the boys have been Brand Reps for several years. One of their first opportunities was with Nike for their Toddler Jordans. We ended up getting connected through a Nike shoot we had done months prior.

3. Was there a particular incident or a series of occurrences that made you begin considering having your boys become Brand Reps / models?
Since they were born they have always had big personalities and seemed to demand attention. And being twins it seems people were always stopping and wanting to take pictures and ask questions. So I said I wanted to try to get them on TV and allow the world to get to know these two amazing little boys.

4. As Brand Reps - what are / were your boy's favorite aspect to reppin'?
Their favorite part has always receiving the free stuff, which was secretly mine too!

5. What steps did you take to convert from Brand Repping to working with a modeling agency?

I started with an agency, which they are still signed to. Being with the agency is what allowed them to tap into Brand Repping.

6. What was the biggest challenge that you faced merging into full-out modeling?

Travel and last minute go-sees. Having a NYC agency and living 4hrs away can be very demanding financially and demanding on time. Having to say no to a job or an audition because of time and finances is very hard. It makes you feel like they are possibly missing out on something that could be actually what's needed to get to the next level.

7. What piece of advice would you share with Brand Rep moms or aspiring moms of models?

To just go for it. Be sure to only sign a flexible contract as having small children anything could change. Also be sure to stay connected with the world through social media, as two of their biggest jobs came directly through social media and not the agency.

8. How old were your boys when they first got signed with Wilhelmina Modeling Agency?

They were just turning five yrs old

9. Do your kids have a favorite modeling experience or have they had any spectacular opportunities that came from their journey as kid models?

I believe their favorite was their recent TV experience. They seem to enjoy becoming someone else and being able to interact with other characters. They were super excited because they know that through that opportunity they are one step closer to being on a Disney show or maybe one of their favorite movies. (They want to be in Transformers lol). One of their opportunities that came was also walking in NY fashion week. Both of these opportunities (TV and NY Fashion week) came directly through social media and not the agency.

10. If you could do it all over again what would you do differently…if anything at all?

I would have started them with an agency a lot sooner.

Expand Your Brand
Reppin' is only the beginning

Throughout this book we have examined the steps taken by the @LivasBoys to grow their social media presence and Brand Reppin' opportunities. You've learned firsthand what Small Shops look for in Brand Reps and you've heard how one mom acquired a modeling contract with one of the top modeling agencies, yet still utilizes the opportunities that Brand Reppin' affords her family.

It's my hope that you will walk away excited about becoming a Brand Rep (or managing the account of your little one). But, don't let the magic stop there. Once you gain a sense of your "Brand Reps" relationship with the camera… begin teaching them about the power of entrepreneurship.

The Kiddie Kitchen Show

Ever since Noah was about 4 years-old, I noticed his love for cooking. Every day after school he would run into the kitchen and say "mommy, I want to help". His brother, Nelson, on the other hand, was more interested in eating whatever he could get his hands on. The dynamics between the two were interesting and definitely entertaining… and it got me to thinking. What would happen if I started filming two toddler boys in the kitchen with a celebrity chef?

Now, my background in media definitely helped me create a show concept and it played an integral role in the execution of the overall show production. But, I believe that there are some things that we typically steer clear of introducing to our kids for one reason or another; either because we think they're too young, they won't understand, or they won't have an interest. But, today I challenge you to be attentive to your child's interests and see if there is a way that your talents or passion can intersect with theirs. That's exactly how the Kiddie Kitchen Show was created.

The Kiddie Kitchen Show launched as a YouTube series in the fall of 2017. Yup, the same year we started Brand Reppin'! To me it was perfect, we had already cultivated an audience now we just had to provide them interesting content... something that would truly capture their attention. So, that meant the cast had to have chemistry and exude fun. We were fortunate to find a chef that had the credentials of a Celebrity Chef and the heart of a kid. Celebrity Chef "E" Marshall is the Head Chef for the cast of FOX's hit show "Empire" and he's the Kiddie Kitchen's favorite Chef. Lastly, the Kiddie Kitchen Jr. Chefs include Chase M, a brilliant and witty 5 year-old and the Livas Boys!

So, what do you get when you put 4 men in the kitchen... 3 of whom are ages 5 and younger?

A real treat! Celebrity Chef "E" takes on the challenge of teaching three Jr Chef's the art of culinary creations every month on The Kiddie Kitchen Show, which will begin airing on a national cable network in April 2018.

Featured left to right: Nelson Livas, Chef "E" Marshall, Chase Monterio and Noah Livas

Now that I've shared what has worked for me, it's your turn to creatively introduce your son or daughter to the wonderful world of entrepreneurship. If you didn't have anyone to teach you how to start a business - don't let that stop you… there are tons of books out there to assist you on your journey. If you already have an idea, but just haven't taken the first step… what are you waiting for… the time is now. I want to leave you with this. If God planted that seed in your mind… it's up to you to manifest it. It may not always be easy, but I promise it will most definitely be worth it.

End of Chapter 8 Questionnaire:

If you're ready to introduce entrepreneurship to your son or daughter, what are some possible business ventures the two of you might enjoy together?

____

____

____

____

____

____

____

____

____

Featured left to right: Noah Livas, Chase Monterio, Nelson Livas

Glossary | References

Brand Representatives
Brand Representatives are individuals contracted to promote a company's products and/or services.

Brand Rep Search
The Brand Rep Search period is determined by individual brands

FB
FB is the acronym for *Facebook*

Follow Loop
Follow Loops utilize a pull strategy for brands/reps that can generate demand through increased visibility, buzz and engagement.

Hashtag
A *hashtag* contains a (#) symbol proceeded by a word or phrase to assist individuals locate posts of interest to them.

- **Common Brand Reppin' Hashtags**
  #brandreppin #brandrep #cutekids #branding #brandrepping #socialmediamodeling #kidmodel #kiddiepreneur #smallshops #marketing #IGkids #IGmodel #brandbuilding #brandenthusiast #followloop #babymodel

IG
IG is the acronym for *Instagram*

Telegram
Telegram is a downloadable app available for Android, iOS, Windows Phone, Windows NT, macOS and Linux.[14] Users can send messages and

exchange photos, videos, stickers, audio and files of any type.

Check out these Telegram Groups by searching the following names (once you download the application): *Social Moms&Dads, The Mom Tribe LIKES, Mummy Likes, ActiveAF*